BACK 2 SCHOOL SUCCESS KIT

IRENE BANGWELL

Published in Nigeria by
Handz and Mindz Ltd
P.O. Box 8531,
Wuse, Abuja
Nigeria

First Edition
First Printing, 2019

ISBN: 978-978-972-423-9

Cover Design
Vodina West
Lakitha Munasinghe

DEDICATION

This book is dedicated to all the outstanding teachers who took my hands and helped me get here.

Especially, Late (Mr.) Antigha Ita Antigha of West African People's Institute, Calabar, Nigeria.

IRENE BANGWELL

BOOK MAP

ACKNOWLEDGMENTS

Taking up projects such as this requires having the right support system; spiritual support system, family support system, office team and friends who cheer you on.

I have been blessed with the gift of strong support system and I have a lot to show for it. I took up a couple of writing projects at the same time including the writing of **Back 2 School Success Kit** and my support system at every point in time, made it possible.

I also want to appreciate parents who have trusted over the years with the mentoring of their children and teenagers. Thank you very much for the many learning opportunities you created for me. Thank you for your faith in me.

I would love to specially thank my fathers of faith for all I have learned from them and how these learning have equipped and shaped me for what God wants of me. I would love to specially appreciate Pastor Andy & Ndidi Osakwe, Drs. Abel & Rachel Damina, Pastor Efezino & Folashade Idheze and Pastors Eshiet & Ofonime Udosen.

I would love to sincerely appreciate, my amazing husband, Kingsley Bangwell. There is no word to describe how blessed I am to have someone who sees what I can be and steadily reminds me to leave my mark in the world. I love you today and always.

I would also love to specially appreciate my brilliant

daughters, Briona and Elena, who made the biggest sacrifice during the time of executing this book writing projects. For this, I appreciate them greatly.

Special thanks to my two foster daughters, Rahab Kumbo and Anurika Okoli, who stepped in, as they always do, to watch the girls and the home-front during these times. I pray that God blesses you greatly and raises help for you as you pursue greatness in your time.

To my amazing, brilliant, resourceful assistant, Sharon Ahumibe, I say, step out there, you have what it takes to live out the best version of your life. Thank you for being so prompt as you typed the manuscripts.

I want to thank Mrs. Olusola Bankole very specially for accepting to write the foreword for this book inspite of her very busy schedule. Your passion for quality education always shines through anytime, any day.

To Mrs. Maureen Ihonor, who generously gave of her time and took the time to write the review that would come to be the afterword of this book, I appreciate you sincerely.

Thank you, Valerie Vishnay & Mordecai Gbaratu, for being amazing and wonderful and patient too.

Thank you to great friends who lent professional help during these times especially Kaiso Dahnyels and Vodina West.

I would also like to say a very big thank you to my amazing mum, Odo Bassey Otu and my brother,

Joshua Essien for their faith in me.

Everyone needs a tag team that believes in them completely and periodically calls them to order, so that one steadily defies the odds and lives out the very best version of their lives. Mine is made up of some of the most amazing people you can imagine. Thank you Mrs Angela Ajala, Mrs. Olusola Bankole, Emem Opashi, Tina Amachree, Kai Orga, Chidiebube Ocheme, Stephanie Itenebe, Wendy Ologe, Viviann Okoye, Rose Ojabo, Inimfon Etuk, Sam Obafemi, Aruk Eteng, Deborah Ikongbeh and so many other amazing people, thank you for your gift of beautiful friendship.

More than eleven years ago, I was so certain that I needed to write but there wasn't that much clarity of what I was going to write. For starters, I just could not get myself to eventually write. The projects I had started, as passionate as I was, I just couldn't bring myself to finish. Till date many of them remain unfinished.

Then Grace happened! Taking me totally on a different journey and pathway than I could ever have thought or imagine. Unprecedented.

Four published works, two manuscript and two outlines later, I have come to return all the glory and honor to the King. Yes, to the maker of times, seasons, graces and places. The one who created me for His own good pleasure, glory and purpose.

Every single thought, insight, knowledge, you would find in these pages are God-breathed. He created all of the events from which I came to draw insights and meaning from.

The strongest memory I have throughout these writing projects is putting pen to paper and just finding words pour out in dimensions I have never thought about. At the weirdest of places and in very awkward moments, I have felt the urge to write and then it just poured out.

I have experienced a divine phenomenon.

This is the Father's time for these learnings. It's been a privilege being a part of this experience.

To the King of Kings and the Lord of Lords, I return ALL of the glory.

Irene Bangwell
Abuja, Nigeria
April 2019

FOREWORD

This is calling out parents and teachers on the need to be deliberate about our roles. Irene shares her life experiences in a manner that produces the Midas effect.

Her ability to weave the story of her life, her journey through school and how she has developed such an awesome dexterity through the support of outstanding teachers, her husband and family is amazing.

I recommend this book to all parents, teachers, students and everyone who need to be outstanding in a task.

Self-awareness, self-regulation, motivation, empathy and social skills are required for effective emotional intelligence which impacts on overall performance.

Irene has shown that these can be learnt and engaged to move a person from the timid, uncoordinated to a confident, organised achiever.

Back 2 School Success Kit is the all-time tool for accomplishing this.

Olusola Bankole
Director, Bankys Private School, Abuja
President, NAPPS (National Association of Proprietors of Private Schools)
PRO, Association of Christian Schools International, North Central Zone.
M.Ed. Guidance and Counselling,
University of Ibadan

ARE WE LOST?
(INTRODUCTION)

A few days ago, I was talking to a friend and in the middle of the conversation he mentioned that he had attended the School of the Gifted, Gwagwalada. Then something inside of me snapped and I almost got emotional. After I left him and for several days after the conversation, I could hardly stop thinking about what my life could have been if I went to a School of the Gifted.

I remember vividly how I wrote the examinations in 1993. My centre was Hope Waddell Training Institution, Calabar. I was 10 years old at the time. My teachers were certain that I would make it, but the results never came out.

Why were they certain?

In moments of self-doubt, I have oftentimes drawn strength from how well I performed academically in Primary School. I happened to have attended Calabar Preparatory International School, Calabar, where I soared and soared and soared. I recall vividly, in 1990, when Nigeria revised the education system to the 6-3-3-4 system. Prior to that school year, first term usually began in January and then the third term was September. I was in primary 2 at the time. I remember my teacher, Ms. Roseline, recounting how I was first for both terms and how I, along with two other girls who had also been doing really well, will be put together in the class of a teacher who was reputed to be a strict but great teacher nonetheless, as we were promoted to Primary 3.

So, we got there and it was a war of brains. In the first term, all three of us came first. It was a tie. By second term, I was the only one who was first and by the third term, I maintained my first position.

Then we got promoted to primary 4 and I was merged again with two boys who had been topping their class and they whooped me a bit. One of them is now a medical doctor with the Nigerian Navy and the other is a US Marine. Primary 4 was hot but I made a comeback. In 1992, then we were in primary 4, our school decided to experiment with giving the mock examinations of the year to Primary 4 and 5. We didn't have a Primary 6. So, we went in for the examinations and I came out best even though I was in primary 4 and we sat for the examination with students in primary 5.

This became the basis for which parents were asked to register their children in Primary 4 for the State and Federal Common Entrance Examinations. I passed the Federal Common Entrance Examination so well, scoring the highest in my school with a score of 520 over 600. This earned me admission into Federal Government Girls' College, Calabar.

I have not been telling this story to gloat. I have been setting the foundation for a story that will sound totally different from how it started.

So, my teachers were confident that I was gifted and passing the School of the Gifted examinations would be a walkover. I wrote the examinations, though.

However, I do not have a memory of the examinations being a walkover. I do not know if I passed or not. I only know that I am not an average student.

I set off for secondary school in September 1993, after turning 10 in July. By my academic records, there was certainty that I would excel. Things very quickly took a downward spiral; that school year was the creepiest school year of my life. I was 10, small, and very naïve.

My seniors took advantage of this and bullied me, and often sent me to run errands that they could not ask my peers who were bolder and older. I was posted to clean toilets and did all kinds of things that I had never done at home. I soon came up with a skin reaction that would make me write my promotional examinations with my left hand. That year, I was promoted on trial.

I was off boarding school for some part of my JSS 2 and JSS 3. In JSS 2, I picked up a bit. I came 19th and then I came 10th. I have almost no memory of JSS 3. I think it's the way my brain helps me cope with times when I get disappointed with life and myself. All I can remember is trying to opt for sciences in SS 1 and I was told that I had failed Mathematics and Integrated Science in Junior WASSCE.

My grandmother, who I had grown up with, was devastated. She was a nurse and so wanted me to be a doctor – specializing in Obstetrics and Gynaecology and unlike most children who did not want to, I loved the idea. So, we went back and forth and the counsellor 'judging by my school results,' said that I was unfit to study sciences. This broke my heart. Then I moved to the D class which was the commercial class.

My mother is an accountant, so it was pretty easy for me. She was around a lot those periods and I gained a lot of confidence and started excelling at school again. Maybe not the top of the class kind of excelling, but I essentially went through with better confidence. I knew I could have 69% average and, on some days, I could have up to 74% average in the 'internal examinations' but I generally never really did well in Mathematics.

In SS 2, I was able to take private Mathematics lessons with Mr. Nnakwe. He was a genius. I could only afford one term of lessons. So, I learned variation. Then we had this Economics teacher, who was a youth corper (NYSC) and she taught us how to solve quadratic equation using graphs. I got it. I understood both and those two topics became the only ones I knew reasonably well in Mathematics.

There were many days that school was a chore for me. I enjoyed Accounts – my mum made sure to explain the concepts to me whenever she was in town. Then SS 3 came. I had an F in Mathematics and a P in English Language.

All hell was let loose at home. But after the hell came private lesson teachers. One of the teachers took me on Mathematics and the other took me on English Language.

Over a three-month period, I had intensive daily lessons in Mathematics and English Language. My Mathematics teacher, Mr. Antigha of blessed memory, was phenomenal. I do not know if he taught the rest of his students in regular classroom settings the way he taught me but he simplified the concepts of Mathematics to my understanding.

He taught me Mathematics in my local dialect. Not only did we get through the mathematics curriculum, he saw to it that I fell in love with the subject and developed a lot of interest in it. As a matter of fact, I did so well that he began to introduce me to Further Mathematics. I loved them both and wanted to learn more.

My English Language teacher, Mr. Solomon was a hacker. He taught as though he was showing one a way out of jail. It was fun, simple and very, very straight to the point.

I rewrote WASSCE and had a C in Mathematics and English. I wasn't satisfied and so I registered for the November/December GCE in 2000 where I had a B2 in Mathematics and a C in English. I remember my centre for that exam, Edgerly Ballantyne Primary School, Calabar.

I may have been the first to finish the last part of the Mathematics exam, when the centre supervisor asked me how it was possible for me to finish Mathematics in such a short time, I didn't know when I asked him if he could take my answer sheet and give me a new one for me to do the examination all over. And boy, I said it with some attitude and he was shocked! Needless to say, he let me go.

This was the same person who was so fearful with an F in mathematics in 1999, but later became confident and with a B2 in Mathematics a year later.

The university days were easy for me. If there was a calculation in a course, there was no way that I would not have an A. I wanted to crack everything possible to understand everything possible. In the first semester of my second year, along with a childhood friend, we wrote a book on a course that students had the prejudice that it was so difficult. Our goal was to simplify it. My first degree is in Banking and Finance and that course was called Mathematics for Finance.

My academic journey is the background for writing this book.

Questions like, "What if Mr. Solomon and Mr. Antigha were my teachers in JSS 3, could I have performed differently in Mathematics? Could I have gone ahead to study science? What if my parents could have afforded to send me to Mr. Nnakwe's lessons from JSS 2? What if I had been a day student at the onset of secondary school? What if I had started a year later?" bug me till this day.

Every day, families and Nigeria as a country lose children with latent ingenuity to circumstances. Circumstances that push people to cope with, settle for, and major in areas that either do not challenge them enough or leave their innate genius untapped.

Think about your painter, your driver, your boss, or your teacher, put in the best of circumstances, is this where they would be? I look around our nation and see that so much is missing and I know that each generation was designed to solve its own problems but when people miss it educationally, they miss how they were supposed to solve the problems they were wired to solve.

Are we lost?

Are you where you are supposed to be?

Can we begin to task ourselves as parents and demand of ourselves to create an ENABLING environment for our children to grow into the best versions of their lives?

Can you do this?

In this book, I talk about an enabling environment from different perspectives; from the perspective of the learner, to that of parents. This book will not tell schools how to run their affairs because it is designed for parents. In this book, you will see what to do for and with your child to bring them to a place of repetitive school success.

CHAPTER ONE
HOW BEHAVIOR SHAPES PERFORMANCE

Typically, parents understand good performance at school to be that children are getting great grades on tests and examinations, while staying out of trouble and being in the best behavior.

In this chapter, I am going to focus the conversation on performance; on learning and getting good grades. Yes, they are two different things entirely. One can stand independent of the other. There are children who are learning but have difficulty expressing it in a way that translates to great grades.

Then there are those who are not learning per se, who are able to take what has been taught, commit it to memory, get by on tests, assignments and end up with grades that parents and teachers are proud of; meanwhile, after the examinations, they have very little memory of the concepts that they so passed in previous examinations. School is about learning and mastery.

I will share loads of ideas on you can work with your child to achieve repetitive well-rounded success.

In the 21st century, parents should be more fixated on mastery, rather than on grades. Fortunately, though, mastery almost always goes with great grades.

Looking at the above paragraph, it is easy to understand that it takes more than a brilliant mind to excel at school. There are many things that lie between learning and grading but I want to focus on the mother of all the factors. Yes, I want to look at one whose influence can be seen prior to learning and all the way to the grading stage.

This factor is 'behavior.' Are you surprised? Students' behavior has an overwhelming influence on their overall school performance. This is where I like to start.

I do understand that schools' methods of assessment can be limited in scope sometimes but, I am writing this book for families, so that their own back end is covered. And I am certain that if behavior issues are addressed, I am certain that children will excel even in a flawed assessment system.

Behavior can be defined as the way in which one acts or conducts him/herself, especially towards others. In the context of education and students in particular, behavior is the manner in which a child acts towards school work which includes academics, general school activities, teachers, students and the school environment.

There are many aspects of activities that make up efforts towards school work and looking at them closely will help us clearly see how student actions, habits in these areas has a significant impact on their overall performance.

Behavior One
School Preparatory Behavior

School preparatory behavior has to do with how a child prepares for the school day. These includes all activities that are carried out in preparation for a school day. Some of the activities begin prior to the school day and have no academic connotations, so they can oftentimes be taken for granted, yet they influence learning outcomes.

Examples of such activities include bedtime, packing of bags to include complete homework, school books needed the next day, cardigans etc., packing of lunch packs to include sufficient water, snacks and food among others.

Leaving homework or notebooks behind means that notes will be copied later, at the time that could have been devoted to rest or reading. Looking at it from a psychological point of view, if your child is consistently leaving something behind at home, they are also leaving important things at school that also affect their readiness for the next day's school work.

If they are also leaving things behind that should aid their comfort, when those things are not available, they become too distracted to learn. Such things may be clothing items or food.

How? If the weather changes and it becomes too cold for instance, a child with no cardigan will be too distracted to pay attention to learn. In the same vein, a child who has not eaten well, perhaps forgot his meal or did not bring in enough food, will be hungry during the course of the day and this can become a source of distraction.

Bedtimes look negligible until they have to be rudely woken up in the morning to catch the school bus. A 2014 study from Tel Aviv University found that just one night of interrupted sleep or startling wake-up was enough to create serious confusion and irritation the next day, and to impact negatively on participants' job performance. The scientists found that interrupted sleep had the same poor consequences for cognition as only getting four hours of sleep a night. Essentially, our brains react very poorly to the idea of being blared out of their rest.

We find that many of our children are up playing games, watching TV up until late and then go to bed really late and have to be woken up suddenly.

It turns out that being wakened suddenly from the rapid eye movement (REM) stage of sleep, which is associated with increased brain activity and dreaming, may actually cause significant mood problems. Mood problems create behavior problems. For instance, a child can easily be disrespectful to a teacher or overreact at a peer.

I recommend allowing games on weekends, having duration-based TV viewing times of about 45 minutes during weekdays and also keeping television out of the children's room altogether. More and more research findings are coming up, showing how this is bad practice and detrimental to the health of the children.

Behavior Two
Homework and Assignment Behavior

Many school children leave their homework until the last minute to work on them and just submit. They call it 'winging it.' This is because they actually believe that homework and assignments are done for the teacher.

Parents need to repeatedly remind their children that homework and assignment are designed to help them (the children) gain mastery.

Mastery means that through homework, children will understand concepts better. They will become fluent with the lesson so much that they can find short cuts in the process. Homework gives opportunity for practice and as the saying goes, practice makes perfect.

Concepts that are taught need to be mastered because of the limited time within which any teacher can teach any subject during regular school hours. So essentially, when our children take their time to do homework, they learn, relearn and master.

Many times, on the next school day, the teacher builds on what was taught previously. The teacher will most likely revise on past concepts but he will also add newer concepts. Where homework was not done properly, the child may not completely understand the newer concepts.

I agree that homework can be a bit bulky, but I do recommend giving reasonable amounts of homework all the same. In fact, I want homework to be notes sent home for review, re-reading and all, for at least two out of five school days. While waiting for schools to make these adjustments, I recommend that the attitude towards homework be one that sees it as a mastery process and not something done for the teacher.

Parents and private lesson teachers need to be careful about doing homework for the children or continually teaching during lessons. This is because homework should leave room for independent study and reflection.

Behavior Three
Note-taking
Note-taking is both an art and a science but prior to the art or the science, there is the act. Many school children do not keep up to date notes. I recall, during the course of my internship, how a father came unannounced to school to check up his son's school work and discovered that even though we were in November and the school term was coming to a wrap, his son's last notes had been taken sometime in September.

A child who does not have up-to-date notes was most likely not in class, will most likely not even know what he was taught and regardless how brilliant he is potentially, cannot consistently do well at school. In preparation for test and examinations, the question I always like to ask is, exactly what are they reading.

Parents should have their children paste their school timetables in their room and periodically, parents should go into the children's rooms and check subjects notes at random.

The art of note-taking, which is the second aspect of note taking, involves careful noting of what is being copied on the board. Some children copy notes randomly without realizing that paragraphs have been skipped or they have copied the note in the wrong order. In the end, many of them copy notes that they will be unable to understand when reading.

The science of note-taking, which is the last aspect of note taking, has to do with writing possibly two notes at the same time; one with a biro and another with a pencil. The biro note-taking involves writing on their normal school notes, what they are formally required to write down as notes, while the one written with a pencil involves writing down key points the teacher is making verbally which may not eventually be part of the main notes. Many teachers speak better than they write.

This implies that when speaking, they will share key anchors for the lesson. Many of these anchors may never make it to the main lesson note.

This means that when speaking, many teachers will share key explanations for the lesson. Many of these explanations may never make it to the meson note but yet they help you understand the entire topic.

A student who has a notepad or journal, where he/she writes key points of the lesson, is most likely to listen more effectively than one who does not. He or she is also most likely to recollect information while reading a lot better than the one who just focused on copying the notes. This is part of the reasons that make absence from class particularly costly. Copying notes alone is not the same as being present when the lesson was taught and taking the notes while it was being dictated.

Behavior Four
In-class Participation

The first aspect of in-class participation involves listening. Listening is active. Listen to hear what the teacher is really saying as well as what they are not. Many students daydream a lot in class. They may be quiet but they are absent in class.

Being distracted in class by friends, phones and pranks, stops them from actually taking in the lesson and, in many cases, missing out salient information that are either part of the lesson or instructions that they would later need to do a particular assignment.

Another important characteristic of in-class participation is asking questions in class. Asking questions during class enables the teacher to address areas of misconceptions. When students do not ask questions, they leave the class with a fog about the lesson. That fog can inhibit comprehension while reading or during subsequent classes.

Behavior Five
Personal Study Behavior

- <u>Reading in bite sizes.</u>

Many students do not even have a personal study habit. They merely read for examinations and tests, and at best, they skim through their notes Many students do not realize that reading notes in bite sizes just after they have been taught enhances mastery of one concept before another is layered on it.

Let us imagine that a certain teacher wants to teach 10 steps to do a particular thing. And so, he or she decides to teach one per lesson. And as it turns out, you have to understand one step before you can understand the next. Attending the class and reading the notes over and over again after the class, not only helps a child understand what has been taught in the past, it also readies him to lean what is to be taught next.

Reading ahead is another level entirely. It allows a student to think through concepts prior to hearing the teacher teach. Using this approach helps a child to come up with questions that can be answered during class, compared to having those questions after the class has been taught.

- <u>Reading to understand.</u>

Apart from the need to read often and consistently in a systemic way, there is also the need to study effectively. Students need to read to understand. Forming the habit of trying to reproduce what they have studied will help a child thoroughly process lesson notes and materials they have been given to study.

After reading, children should attempt to summarize lessons by writing summaries, drawing mind maps, discussing with peers and recording voice notes of their lessons. This has proven to be very effective.

Here is a typical mind map:

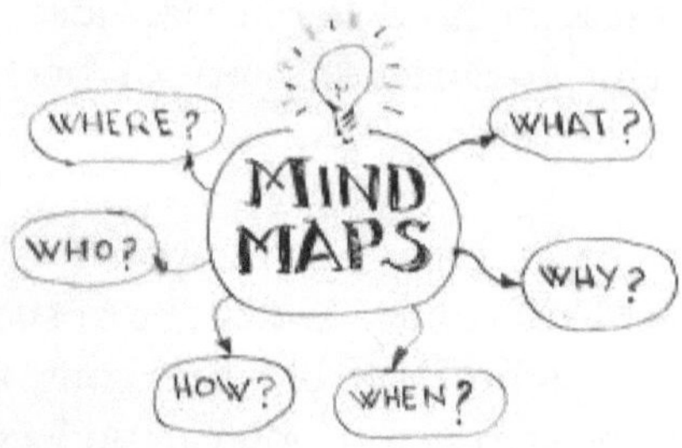

A mind map allows a child figure out the most important parts of the lesson as well as the key information.

When it comes to using mind maps as a study tool, they are useful for organizing thoughts in new ways. They help us see how things are structured and connected. The process of developing mind maps requires a student to develop one sentence summaries from large chunks of notes. It is in the process of summarizing that they master the concepts.

- <u>Using schedules and time table.</u>
I recommend that children have a reading schedule that allots time effectively between subjects. Subjects that have more notes and require more than reading (e.g. calculation, building, etc.) should be given a higher amount of time than those which require reading and comprehension alone. I recommend two to three

hours of study each day.

A parent can ask, what about children who close at say 6pm, when does he/she get to finish homework, read and then go to bed at a good enough time to be ready for school the next day.

My recommendation would be, as a parent review holistically. See where you can cut down a bit on lessons. Or totally reorganize lessons to be about supervising after school studies. Sometimes the academics become and overload and slows down the child as a result.

Periods of study can be interjected with short walks, bathroom breaks, etc. The location where the study happens should be suitable in terms of space, lighting and adapted to a child's learning style. You would learn more on learning styles later on in the book.

Behavior Six
Written Work Behavior

Written work refers to a child's actual writing that is usually submitted for grading. This can be broken into pre-assessment and post assessment behavior.

<u>Pre-assessment behavior</u> involves how a child writes during test, assignment, homework, etc. 'How' here includes: how the writing is done in terms of legibility and what is written in the course of the writing.

Writing legibly involves writing in an organized manner and neatly. Many school children write hurriedly, cancel a lot and their handwriting is not legible enough. Many teachers cannot read their handwriting. This has nothing to do with writing the right answers or not. Yet, it influences their score on the average.

There are teachers who come to understand their handwriting or may not mind straining to read it. But, the idea of straining to read a child's work does something to the score line. It's not the same as when it is legible. Please note that legible is not the same as cursive handwriting. Legibility does not necessarily mean it is beautiful It just means that it is easy to read. Some children have beautiful handwriting that is difficult to read.

Some other students write legibly but in a disorganized manner. They also write hurriedly and, in many cases, do not pay attention to read the questions properly in order to understand what is being asked. So, they may know the answers but because they did not read the questions to the point of understanding what was being asked, they misfire in their responses and so they get the answers wrong and earn low grades for it.

Some children are sloppy and careless, and sometimes submit their work without having their names written on their answer sheet It is not every time a mistake happens that it should be considered sloppiness or carelessness. If a child has the habit of making a specific mistake, his or attention needs to be drawn to it.

On pre-assessment behavior, you also have children

who know the answers but have two problems with their communication. The first has to do with spellings, punctuation and grammar. They know the answers but now cannot communicate. The second has to do with using the allocated time for test and examinations well.

On issues regarding spellings, punctuation and grammar, many parents have often times said that grammar is not the true test of knowledge. Many children have bought into these kinds of thinking. These sayings are not exactly true. English may be a language that appears to be unrelated to intelligence but it is a tool for demonstrating understanding and knowledge especially in the classroom.

Children need to be taught about the value of English Language as a subject on the curriculum. They need to know that English Language cross cuts into about every subject in the curriculum.

Therefore, it should not be taken for granted. Homework, assignment and project work that involve doing research and essays should be treated with utmost importance, not just for the grades but with the understanding that English Language is a skill building subject. This is the first place to start.

Secondly, to build a child's vocabulary – which is a child's choice of words in written and spoken communication, children have to spend time reading non-academic books.

Children who read a lot of novels will most likely spell better than children who do not. Children who read more are very imaginative and will have the words to express their ideas or answers in both essays in English Language and other subjects as well.

Many examination questions require children to provide answers in their own understanding. Children with a rich vocabulary will always outperform their peers with a limited vocabulary.

On how students use time during examinations, we need to address issues around examination tension and fears. Many students get nervous and confused for the first few minutes on arrival into the test or examination hall. This throws them off and makes pulling themselves together to answer questions difficult.

The real question is why are they nervous? The first reason would be that they do not feel prepared enough for the examinations. So, I ask, what does prepare enough mean?

Prepare enough here means, reading through everything that was taught to the point of understanding the several topics that may have been taught.

In essence, they have not covered the subject content, they are afraid that they may not write well enough, they are concerned that the teacher may not mark them fairly, they are under the examination hype, etc.

We have to address this in the most practicable way possible. Examination is overhyped. We should see examinations as a means for teachers to assess how much of what they taught that a student has mastered. If children attend lessons, ask questions in class, read after every lesson, do homework and essentially review what has been taught, then they would be ready for examinations; especially if grammar-based barriers have been eliminated.

Periodic test and homework can be used to serve as pointers for whether students are really learning and following what has been taught. This is why cheating or copying, misleads a teacher into thinking that students has mastered a given concept.

Take for instance, a teacher gives a test to a class and 80% fail this test. Maybe its safer to use classwork. So, lets say 80% fail this classwork. That would force a teacher to re-teach.

Let me use a true life experience to buttress this. A few months ago, my friend had a concern of her son coming home with a mathematics homework that the young man could not wrap his head around. She knew how to solve the mathematics but soon realized that her son could not grasp it. She tried to teach him but to no avail. Then she was faced with two options of what to do. One was to just write it out for him to copy, the other was to take the homework to school undone.

What would you have done?

She took the homework to school undone. Asked to meet the mathematics teacher and explained to him her son's difficulty in grasping the concept. The teacher thanked her and said, he noticed the struggle of the children and he had mentioned to the head teacher that the concept may have been inappropriate for their age.

Can you beat that?

Sending our children to school is actually a partnership. We should provide feedback to the school about our children at the individual level. We are not supposed to assume that the school knows it all. Neither should we, in the name of meeting school standards cause our children more harm in the name of 'helping' them.

If homework is done well and even left undone when it proves difficult, then teachers get the feedback to reteach. By the time children are preparing for test or examinations, it will be over concepts that they have truly mastered and there would be no need for the anxiety that comes with examinations. School success is predictable.

In mentoring teens, I always tell them that they can actually predict the final scores. This is based on the fact that examination grades are not responsible for their total grades. Final subject grades are based on a build-up. Their completed notes are marked as assessment. They do class tests in a predictable manner. Meaning that they can be prepared.

Many teachers hint about their test. Those who do not, still give hints that they may give impromptu tests. Many school calendars have assessment week, which essentially points to the fact that continuous assessment will most likely hold during a certain week. Unfortunately, some children/school students still show up on those days unprepared.

What this means is that a student's grades are a combination of tests, assignments and marked notes before examinations. Many of the questions answered in the course of tests, assignments and projects are usually also part of the examination questions.

Finally, students need to be taught that reading only when it is time for examinations is unrealistic. Let us imagine that they get a two weeks' notice prior to examinations and they offer 9 subjects with an average of 40 pages of notes. First and foremost, many of them will not read until 4 days, or even less, to the examinations. And what that means is that many subject notes will be opened for the first time during the week of the examinations. Some will be read just four hours before time and not as much comprehension can be done when there is tension.

The tension they feel prior to examination is controllable. Subjects that they are better prepared for are approached with less fear. Indeed, it is often said that 'examinations are not the true test of knowledge' but I dare add that 'examinations are not the true test of capacity' but they are the 'true test of readiness'.

Behavior Six
Post Assessment Behavior
This has to do with a child's attitude towards his returned script after marking. We have emphasized grades a whole lot and at the expense of learning. As a result, the average school child basically checks what their scores are on a test and moves on. There is a poor

post-test review culture.

This is the culture of checking to see teachers' remarks on their scripts, questions they scored poorly on and writing out the correct answers as well as questions they scored highly on, to learn from how they may have answered those questions.

The average person, especially here in our climes, is not scientific. It's easier to make assumptions than to identify patterns, trends or study relationships between things.

It is easier to make hasty conclusions about how the teacher is miserly with marks, is mean. It is also easy to be more interested in who scored the highest and even buy the idea that they may not be good enough or talented enough to do well in a particular subject. The smart thing to do is to reflect and review after an event has taken place.

We build this culture if we steadily remind, demand of our children to reflect and review on their past scripts. Let us begin to down play what they scored and begin to ask questions like, which question did you score the highest, which did you score lowest, which was wrong, have you found what the answer is, what did your teacher comment on the script etc.

When our children begin to find the answers to those questions, they would have been learning how to recreate success.

Behavior Seven
Response to Rigor
I have spent the last decade working with different stakeholders on making classrooms more engaging. I have sought to see how our curriculum can be more hands-on and adapted to children's learning style, can be 21st century relevant and ensure character development.

In the course of doing this, one would think that we are trying to make school easy. School is not designed to be easy. School is a place for self-discovery and birthing genius. That means children would be stretched outside of their comfort zones. A great school ignites children and pushes them to do what they would ordinarily not believe they could.

This does not mean overworking the child physically or laboring; this means carefully designing learning content that opens a child to a lot more knowledge about their world, while also instilling in them a sense of personal responsibility.

For instance, a normal school will teach 'Care of clothes' as a list of things to do to keep our clothes clean. A good school will teach how to read labels on clothes in order to know what kind of care each material needs. But a great school will teach all of the above plus how to detect what a material is and why certain care should be given to those materials.

It will be easier to write a list and get an A, compared to learning clothing labels icons, and then having to make a chart to show what each icon represents.

Perhaps, it will be a lot tougher to create a chart of clothing materials, list what they are made of and what kinds of care each of them needs.

School should be rigorous but the rigor should be met with an excitement in a child that he or she is about to make discoveries.

There are several efforts being put in place to make rigor fun and rewarding for children and I believe they are yielding efforts regardless of the pace.

Many of our children have an irrational fear of rigor. Once a task, assignment or question is not something they have heard about before, or something they can easily find in their text books or note books, they quake, fear, copy, and look for an escape. Yes, they dock. Meanwhile, this is the real point of learning. Many children dock throughout their years in school, picking only subject content that have surface interactions. No depths, no true meaning, no innate ingenuity birth in the process.

I recall a classmate of mine in the university. He was out of this world in his approach to assimilating. He asked the weirdest questions. Many times, I tuned out when he asked those questions. There were times that I would try to make a connection between what he was saying and what was taught, and it just did not sit well with me.

Later on, I realized that first off, he usually read ahead. Secondly, he was not afraid to interact with difficult or rigorous concepts. A few years ago, when I learned that he was back at the university to teach, I thought he would be a big blessing to his students.

What should the response be when a student comes across materials that seem rigorous, difficult and scary?

What should students do when they are asked questions that have different kinds of answers and needs their opinion? What should students do when the answer is not at the back of the text book?

Step One
Rewrite the question in the exact same way the teacher wrote it.

Step Two
Underline the key words and phrases used in framing the questions.

Step Three
Pick the key words and phrases and try to identify what each of them means in relation to the question.

Step Four
Rewrite the entire question in their own words, substituting their own interpretation of the key words and phrases.

Step Five

Write a two-paragraph summary of what was taught previously on the subject matter or relating to the subject matter.

Step Six

Write out any special additional instructions that were given along with the assignment, whether written or verbal.

Step Seven

Write a to-do list on the task that was given. This would involve going through previous steps and identifying what you think you are required to do.

Step Eight

You can take a step further by doing something extra that will make their work unique.

Step Nine

Now start carrying out all the task you have listed in step seven.

Here's an example:
To make the best of this, children should read the example over and over again.

School project task

Mary and Martha are not happy with each other today. Mary accused Martha of discoloring her white school uniform. What can Martha do at another time to avoid discoloring her sister's clothes and even her own clothes?

Draw a chart that Martha and Mary can hang up in their room to guide them at another time they need to do their laundry.

Solution:

Step One

Mary and Martha are not happy with each other today. Mary accused Martha of discoloring her white school uniform. What can Martha do at another time to avoid discoloring her sister's clothes and even her own clothes?

Step Two

Mary and Martha are <u>not happy</u> with each other today. Mary accused Martha of <u>discoloring</u> her <u>white school uniform</u>. What can Martha do next time to <u>avoid discoloring</u> her sister's clothes and even her own clothes?

Step Three

Discoloring – Color of a dress has changed in the course of washing.

White school uniform – white uniform now has a new color. White uniform is made from cotton.

Avoid discoloring – Wash clothes of multiple colors in such a way that they do not discolor each other.

Step Four

Mary and Martha are sisters. Mary helped Martha wash her white school uniform that is made of cotton. She may have washed it together with another dress of a different color and that color stained the white uniform. What does Martha need to know about washing white cotton materials with clothes of other colors?

Step Five

Ms. Asari has taught us about how different materials respond to different kinds of detergent. She has taught us about how white clothes must never be washed with other colors. She has also taught us on how materials that are color-fast should be washed.

We are draw up a fabric care chart for Mary and Martha.

Step Six

She mentioned that the chart must be colorful and no more than one page of plain sheet.

Step Seven

I am required to:

- List steps to be taken when washing colors.
- List steps for washing cotton materials.
- List steps for washing whites.

Step Eight

To make my work unique, I will also:

- Do quick reminders at different points of the sheet.
- Create 'yes' and 'no' icons.
- Laminate my own finished work.

Step Nine

To do the task, I will look at my notes, look at my text

books and get on Google.

And that does it. It should really be fun doing it.

Usually I recommend that children who have arts flare or anything unique, always use it to spice up their project work.

Rigorous tasks when broken down can be a whole lot easier to carry out. In breaking down tasks, students are able to identify what is required, what they need, what they have and where they need help. Being quick to tag along with friends who eventually get to do the task is not always helpful unless the student devotes the time to actually learn how the task is done to the point that they learned from the process.

All of these play a key role in shaping academic performance and will continue to make a big difference.

- **Key Points**

- School success is measured by two factors: learning and then grades. The two must go together.
- Behavior has a strong influence on both learning and grades.
- If a child attends lessons, ask questions, reads after each class, does his or her homework properly, prepares for test and examinations, writes legibly and brilliantly, then success will be their reward.
- School children should be taught how to manage the panic that comes every time they approach a seemingly difficult school task.

CHAPTER TWO
NON-BEHAVIOR INFLUENCES OF SCHOOL PERFORMANCE

In the previous chapter, I explained at length the different factors that make up for behaviour influences on school performance. In this chapter, I will be looking at non-behavior influence of school performance. Many times, non-behaviour influences are the backend drivers of behaviour influences.

I recommend that parents pay really close attention as I identify these factors as well as how to manage them.

Non-behavior one
Intrinsic Motivation

This refers to the motivation to engage in a behavior arising from within an individual because they find such behavior naturally satisfying to them. In the context of education and school performance, intrinsic motivation refers to a situation in which a child takes school work seriously because they place value on their educational experience.

The opposite of intrinsic motivation would be extrinsic motivation, which in this case would be about a child putting in effort at school, taking school seriously because of what they would get as a reward from their parents. For some children, this form of motivation may come because their parent may have promised to reward them with things such as a vacation, money, ice cream treat, take them swimming etc., if they scored certain grades.

While extrinsic motivation can make a difference, in my experience, I have found intrinsic motivation more enduring. Sometimes, we can start out using extrinsic motivation and overtime the motivation may become intrinsic.

In practical terms, what does intrinsic motivation look like? I have had experience fostering four teenagers thus far. I have seen how children who 'want' to go to school, who 'have a goal' for why they should be in school, respond to school work. You are not likely to remind them to read, copy notes, prepare early to leave for school, etc. Almost certainly, it always shows in their scores/grades.

Children who do not place value on school are not as eager. School deadlines may not mean much to them. They are very quick to make excuses or blame someone else. It takes almost nothing for them to miss classes or say they don't want to go to school on a given day. When you have children or teens who don't place value on school, you would soon find that you as an adult, are more passionate about their school success.

It's funny that sometimes, children who go through unique forms of hardship are most likely to be intrinsically motivated. Even though, this is not always the case.

I have seen children not respond to school because someone in their space has a strange belief about the value of education. For instance, female children growing up in certain communities consider success in life to be meeting a man who marries them and picks their bills. Unfortunately, school grades do not contribute in any way to meeting a rich man and so, they go through the motions of school as if it were a chore.

In summary, the importance that children ascribe to school will determine their own efforts and the results they get.

Non-behavior two
Inappropriate Class by Age

Nigeria currently has a situation in hand with parents moving children far too quickly and too early from primary school to secondary school. Children are moving into secondary school as early at the ages of 8 and 9. Many parents do this for different reasons including the child's brilliance, cost of fees and just general disregard for Primary Six amongst other reasons which may or may not include the need to have their children graduate at a certain age. Many parents want their children to graduate and get into the labour market early.

Some of these reasons seem legitimate on the face value; however, it does not take into consideration the child's overall well-being. Let me expand a bit on moving children to secondary school on the basis that they are excelling academically.

Some parents say that their children are doing so well academically and so in their estimation the child can handle secondary school academic rigor. First and foremost, secondary school involves more than academic capabilities. The school work is more psychologically demanding than it is academically.

Teachers are not designed to be as patient as those in primary school. There are no teachers sitting through the school day in the class with the students. So, teachers do not track their progress, challenges, etc., as used to be the case in primary school. Children at this level need to drive their academics at a personal level. They need to be self-driven, self-appraising, etc.

In primary school, they had one teacher sitting through the course of the school day with them. Who most likely taught them about everything except for maybe languages and where specialized teachers taught Mathematics and English Language. Secondary school is totally different. They have to in many cases move from venue to venue. They may not even be noticed should they be absent. Thus, incentivising irresponsible behaviour.

A brilliant child can get into secondary school and be lost. Lost to indiscipline, confusion, bullying, peer influences that undermine his or her concentration and attitude towards school work.

In secondary school, when a child does not understand a concept, the class does not stop. Concepts are not repeated in the ways they are in primary school. Every secondary school day is connected to the external exams. So, when a child falls back, it has long term impact.

Younger secondary school students are more susceptible to caving into the overwhelm. Some of them never recover. As I write this, beyond statistics, I have names and faces of peers that caved in to the pressure. Are we lost?

In the case that you find you have a gifted child who is a genius (meaning that they have exceptional abilities that are largely uncommon), please research on the best ways to support your child. This might require that you send the child outside of Nigeria to school environments that are designed for children with their abilities. Nigeria may not at the moment have the school environment for your child's kind.

Secondary school requires a combination of several factors other than academic prowess which in itself can cave in, in the face of the other factors. Stability and maturity are the core factors for school success in Secondary education. I recommend that children, regardless of their academic abilities, turn 11 before heading to secondary school.

At 11, they would need a great amount of support. One year prior to starting secondary school, they will need to start building routines around self-leadership which will include preparing themselves for school, hygiene, managing school work, self-appraisal, etc. Essentially, it is within this period that they can build the necessary awareness and skills that are needed to thrive in an independent learning environment.

Beginning these kinds of routines at 10, may wear down a child in combination with school work.

Here is what is applicable in other secondary school systems across the globe.

As part of education in the **United States**, the definition of secondary education varies among school districts but generally comprises grade 7 (age 12–13).

In **England and Wales**, pupils aged between 12 and 13 are in Year 8 which is the second year of Secondary School. The Scottish equivalent is Secondary 1 or S1 - the first year of Secondary education. The **Northern Irish** equivalent is Year 9 or Second Form, the second year of secondary education. It is rare for pupils younger than 12-13 to enter Year 8.

In **Hong Kong**, pupils aged 12 to 13 are in Secondary 1 or Form 1, the first year of secondary education.

In some states of **Australia** including Victoria, New South Wales, Queensland, Australian Capital Territory, and Tasmania, Year 7 is the first year of secondary school, but it is actually the eighth year of schooling (Prep/Kindergarten, 1 through 6, then Year 7). In Australia, Year 7 students are aged 12–13 years old.

The **Irish** equivalent to seventh grade is First Year, which is the first year of secondary education. Students are usually 12-13 years old.

In **Iran,** Grade 7 is the first year of Highschool A. There are 2 stages of Highschool in Iran: A and B. A ranges from grade 7 to 9 and B ranges from 9 to 12. Most of Iranian 7 graders are 13 years old.

In **Belgium and the Netherlands**, the 7th grade is similar to the "eerste klas" or "brugklas" (Transition class) in the Netherlands, and "1e middelbaar" or "1ière secondaire" in Belgium. It's the first year of high school. When reaching the age of 12/13, the children go from primary school ("basisschool") to high school ("middelbare school").

In **Brazil,** the time to be spent in elementary school was recently raised from eight years to nine years, and the minimum age required to enter the seventh grade was not changed. The students are usually between 11 and 13.

In **Bulgaria**, it would correspond to седми клас or 7-ми клас. Students are usually 13 years old.

In the **Philippines,** Grade 7 is the first year of Junior High School. Students are usually 12–13 years old.

In **South Africa,** Grade 7 is the final year of primary school and is also the final year before High School as there is no such thing as Middle School in South Africa. Pupils (called Learners by the Department of Education) are usually between the ages of 11, 12 and 13.

In **Norway**, students enter the seventh grade the year they turn 12 years old. This is the final year of Barneskole (literally Kids School), equivalent to Elementary School.

In **New Zealand**, Year 8 (formerly Form 2) is the equivalent of seventh grade, with students aged 12 or 13 during the year. It is the eighth and final year of primary school and the eighth year of compulsory education.

In **Singapore**, seventh grade is called Secondary One, and it is the start of one's secondary education after one completes primary education. Pupils are typically at the age of 13 in seventh grade.

In **Saudi Arabia,** seventh grade is the first year of Middle School. Students are required to be between 12 and 13 years old.

Grade 7 in **Canada** is the first year of intermediate school, junior high school, or the last grade of elementary school. Pupils are aged 12 by this class.

In **Greece,** seventh grade is called 1st year of middle school (1η γυμνασίου in Greek). It is the first year of Greece's middle school (γυμνάσιο). Students are typically aged 12 – 13.

In **Israel,** in most formal places, the seventh grade is the first year of middle school. Students are typically aged 12.

In **Russia,** students in seventh grade are usually 12–14 years old.

In **Malaysi**a, the seventh grade can be referred to as Form 1. It is the beginning of student's secondary school after completing primary school at the age of 13.

These countries can not all be wrong.

I do know that one of the influences for taking children out to secondary school a lot earlier, especially for big kids, is how they look in uniforms. In which case, it will not be wrong to also consider it as a perception management problem.

One thing schools can begin to do is to reorganize around this class. Choosing prefects from this class can help change the perception. I also have this idea that curriculum content for this class should become a hybrid of primary and secondary school structure. So that it essentially becomes a secondary school readiness class.

I also recommend to parents to sign their children up for possible gap year programs after primary 5 that prepare them academically, psychologically and psychosocially for secondary school in the absence of a Primary 6 class in your children's school.

Non-behavior Three
The 21st century has brought with it the death of the siesta.

Afternoon naps are gone. Some schools have students getting home at 6pm and some have homework and will sleep late and get up the next day. Guess what? We are already running adult routines for them. This will surely have an impact on their health at the end of the day. This can fog their sense of judgement, memory retention and make them constantly irritable which can also lead to behavior problems at school as a result of them misjudging their current realities.

What should you do?

Help them get as much rest as possible.

In 2015, the National Sleep Foundation came up with an update on the recommended hours of sleep for persons of all ages:

- New-borns (0-3 months): Sleep range is 14-17 hours each day
- Infants (4-11 months): Sleep range is 12-15 hours
- Toddlers (1-2 years): Sleep range is 11-14 hours
- Pre-schoolers (3-5): Sleep range is 10-13 hours
- School age children (6-13): Sleep range is 9-11 hours.
- Teenagers (14-17): Sleep range is 8-10 hours
- Younger adults (18-25): Sleep range is 7-9 hours
- Adults (26-64): Sleep range is 7-9 hours
- Older adults (65+): Sleep range is 7-8 hours

"This is the first time that any professional organization has developed age-specific recommended sleep durations based on a rigorous, systematic review of the world scientific literature relating sleep duration to health, performance and safety," said Charles A. Czeisler, PhD, MD, chairman of the board of the National Sleep Foundation, chief of sleep and circadian disorders at Brigham and Women's Hospital, and Baldino Professor of Sleep Medicine at the Harvard Medical School.

Non-behavior Three
Mental Health Issues in Children and Teens

One of the most life changing experiences I have ever had in the course of my work was when I had the opportunity to interact with five teenagers in SS 2 and SS 3 during the course of my post graduate studies. I had oftentimes talked about how mental health influences academic performance but quite frankly, it took doing those sessions for me to come face to face with the truth that, as parents, our children's states of mind are very crucial to their success in school and elsewhere.

There are many factors that contribute to healthy or unhealthy states of mental health and I will talk about them below:

a.   Children's health and nutrition

School work requires energy and good nutrition to drive it. Many school children do not eat well before coming to school and do not have really nutritious meals in their packs. As a result, we find that many of them get tired easily, fall sick often and even end up missing classes.

Generally, they are not as strong. Parents with picky eaters need to find a way to augment. Meanwhile, in the long term, they become conscious of how thin they look and if as a result they have stunted growth, all of that eats them up emotionally.

Findings have revealed that malnutrition affects physical growth, cognitive development and it consequently impacts on academic performance, health and survival of learners.

b.   Family finances

Students who had less pocket money than their friends were ashamed of the homes they lived in or what clothes they wore, and they spent a lot of time in school feeling inferior.

I cannot live my life as a parent trying to outspend other parents of my children's friends but I can teach my children gratitude and contentment. I can make them see that I am committed to them. Spending time and forging meaningful relationships with our children definitely helps them process these disparities better.

c. Participation in social activities

Many students are so withdrawn from school activities and many times this comes from a place of being overly conscious of their bodies. They have a low self-esteem, do not see themselves as capable and so on and so forth.

Some are able to pour their energies into their academics but some are not. They feel just the same way about their capabilities in academics. They believe they are incapable of success.

d. Romantic inclinations

Some students have been exposed far too early to sexual relationships. At this level, I am talking about peer sexual relationships, which by the way is still illegal. Unfortunately, they are minors and can hardly process the emotions that arise in the aftermath.

I once read about a 14-year-old who reached out to a counsellor to say that she was tired of having sex.

e. Outright sexual abuse

Some children are being sexually abused right under their parent's roof by relatives and neighbours.

Child sexual abuse includes touching and non-touching activity. Some examples of touching activity include:

- touching a child's genitals or private parts for sexual pleasure

- making a child touch someone else's genitals, encouraging a child to play sexual games or have sex putting objects or body parts (like fingers, tongue or penis) inside the vagina, mouth or in the anus of a child for sexual pleasure

- inappropriate sexual touching of a child, whether clothed or unclothed

- penetrative sex

Some examples of non-touching activity include:

- showing pornography to a child

- deliberately exposing an adult's genitals to a child

- photographing a child in sexual poses

- encouraging a child to watch or hear sexual acts

- not taking measures to protect a child from witnessing sexual activity or images

- possessing images of child pornography

- forcing a child to strip or masturbate

- engaging in any kind of sexual activity in front of a child, including watching pornography

- inappropriately watching a child undress or use the bathroom

What are the signs that a child is being abused?

The child says he or she is being touched inappropriately. If a child can tell his or her parents as soon as it begins, we are half way through the healing process.

Even if you had suspected that your child was doing something wrong consensually before, if they raise a concern, please do not ignore it. Neither should you also ignore the so-called 'consensual' sex that may be going on between two minors or even those that involve an adult. Fight for your child. Until they are 18, they do not have the best judgement on these kinds of issues.

Children often show us rather than tell us that something is upsetting them. There may be many reasons for changes in their behavior, but if we notice a combination of worrying signs it may be time to call for help or advice.

- Acting out in an inappropriate sexual way with toys or objects.

- Nightmares, sleeping problems.

- Becoming withdrawn or very clingy.

- Becoming unusually secretive.

- Sudden unexplained personality changes, mood swings and seeming insecure.

- Regressing to younger behaviors, e.g. bedwetting, wetting and soiling accidents that are unrelated to potty training.

- Persistent or recurring pain during urination and bowel movement.

- Unreasonable fear of particular places or people.

- Outburst of anger.

- Changes in eating habits.

- New adult words for body parts and no obvious source.

- Talk of a new, older friend and unexplained money or gifts.

- Self-harm (cutting, burning or other harmful activities).

- Physical signs, such as, unexplained soreness or bruises around genitals or mouth, sexually transmitted diseases, pregnancy, etc.

- Running away.

- Not wanting to be alone with a particular child or young person.

Any one sign does not mean that a child was or is being sexually abused, but the presence of several warning signs suggests that you should begin to ask questions and consider seeking help. Keep in mind that some of these signs can emerge at other times of stress such as:

- During a divorce.

- Death of a family member or pet.

- Problems at school or with friends.

- Other anxiety-inducing or traumatic events.

Signs That an Adult May Be Using Their Relationship with a Child for Sexual Reasons

The signs that an adult may be using their relationship with a child for sexual reasons may not be obvious. We may feel uncomfortable about the way they play with the child, or seem always to be favouring them and creating reasons for them to be alone. There may be cause for concern about the behavior of an adult or young person if they:

- Refuse to allow a child sufficient privacy or to make their own decisions on personal matters.

- Insist on physical affection such as kissing, hugging or wrestling even when the child clearly does not want it.

- Are overly interested in the sexual development of a child or teenager.

- Insist on time alone with a child with no interruptions.

- Spend most of their spare time with children and have little interest in spending time with people their own age.

- Regularly offer to babysit children for free or take children on overnight outings alone.

- Buy children expensive gifts or give them money for no apparent reason.

- Frequently walk in on children/teenagers in the bathroom.

- Treat a particular child as a favourite, making them feel 'special' compared with others in the family.

- Pick on a particular child.

Sources: Parents Protect, UK & NHS UK.

Other causes of mental health issues include:

f. Domestic violence

Children whose parents steadily fight are steadily anxious. They hardly have a restful night and they come to school with a hangover of a cocktail of emotions.

Due to the atmosphere at home, their body produces a hormone called adrenaline in unhealthy doses.

The adrenaline is designed to help us cope in stressful situations, but when produced too often, can lead to its production when there is no danger. Its overproduction and production where there is no danger is very unhealthy for any human being, talk more of a child.

Side effects that come with it include light headedness, blurry vision, and nervousness all of which create a state of mind that makes it near impossible for a child to learn or recall what they have read.

When parents fight, kids feel stranded. They feel like they are lost in a desert. The sense of helplessness is crazy.

g. Bullying

Bullying is the other side of domestic violence. This could be happening at school.

While domestic violence can sometimes be directed at a child; however, it mostly involves parents and the child is mostly a spectator. Bullying on the other hand is directed at the child and has long term effects on a child's self-esteem. If happening at school, a child will not fully participate in school related activities - academic or non-academic alike.

And sometimes, kids are being bullied at home such that while their parents may not be fighting, someone in their home is making life unbearable.

Can you relate? Did this ever happen to you in your childhood?

There are things parents can do to nip this in the bud and they include:

• <u>Give your children a voice at home.</u> If they can speak up at home, then they are most likely to speak up at school or whenever someone at home tries to intimidate them.

• <u>Have a relationship with your children that allows them speak to you when they have misbehaved.</u> That way, you disarm people who may attempt to blackmail them.

I once read about a father who had his son drop him off at a conference. Afterwards, his son was to go fix the car and they had estimated the time that it will take along with the time he would wrap up at the conference. It so happened that the son may have finished a little bit earlier and went to the cinema to watch a movie. By the time the movie was over, he realized his dad may have been waiting.

While waiting, the father called his mechanic, who mentioned that he had finished a lot earlier. By the time, the young man arrived to pick his dad, he lied that the mechanic had taken a little more time.

Guess what his father did?

His father was heartbroken that he had raised his son to believe that it was better to lie than to face him with the truth.

Do not only demand for your children to speak truth. Give them no reason to tell you lies.

Disarm the people that want to blackmail your children.

<u>Encourage sharing and do a lot of listening.</u> While not trying to turn your children into gossips, create room for them to tell you about the things they are uncomfortable with.

When you are back from work, talk about how your day went and ask them to share how theirs went.

Also, be alert and quick to observe changes. Please do not become paranoid in the process. Just be alert.

While behavior may depend largely on a child, non-behavior influences of performance provides parents the opportunity to offer proactive support to the children.

- **Key Points**

- What adults say, in front of children, about education or about life in relation to education influences the value that children will place on their education.
- The recommended age for transiting to secondary school is 11.
- Children need to sleep for a lot longer duration at night to be refreshed enough for school. Having bedtime rules is highly recommended.
- Build a listening relationship with your children. Do not only demand for your children to speak truth. Give them no reason to tell you lies and in so doing, you will also disarm the people who would want to blackmail them.

CHAPTER THREE
SETTING SCHOOL GOALS THAT WORK

Every time we hear about success at school as parents, all we tend to see is the finish line. Yep! Finish lines such as WASSCE, BECE, IGCSE, Checkpoint, JAMB, IELTS, TOEFL and even basic termly and even promotional examinations. This, for us as parents, is how we measure success. School success, as with success in various parts of our lives, does not happen by accident but requires certain building blocks from both parents and their children.

In this chapter, I talk about the building blocks for success. From setting goals to what makes achieving it possible.

The first step to achieving anything of significance is setting goals. For many of us parents, goals-setting is usually something we demand of the child. It is the children that sit down and pen something down and then bring it for us to take a look, if we even do that at all. In all fairness, our children usually write to the best of what they know and to fulfill righteousness. Many times, what is written as a goal becomes just another sheet of paper that we may never take a look at until the last day of the school year when the final results are out.

What makes for effective school goal setting?

It has to be realistic.

For starters, when it comes to setting school goals, the major word to remember as a guide is the word 'REALISTIC'. With school goals, we have to keep it realistic.

How do we measure realistic?

1. Our expectations have to be in line with the school's curriculum and provided scheme of work. Many times, what we expect our children to be able to do at certain ages and what we expect them to have learned, may not even be in their scheme of work.

   Parents need to pay attention to the scheme of work usually given to provide an insight into what children will be learning over a period of time.

   Some schools issue a one-page document showing the planned school work for the term, while others give elaborate subject by subject planned school work.

2. A child's pace is a critical factor in goal-setting. Therefore, two children should not be expected to set the same goals. One child's goal of a Credit (C) in a particular subject can be just as good as another child's goal of an A in the same subject.

A child's pace and individuality should always be factored in.

3. School goals should not be overwhelming. A child who had a few Cs should not be allowed to write 8As as their goal for the year. It could result in one of two things: they could either be overwhelmed with the burden of work or quit as a result of fatigue, or they may totally ignore the goal. Either ways, they are not set on the path of progress.

4. Setting goals without provision for adult and especially parental supervision is equal to unrealistic. When school goals are set, parents must demonstrate readiness to supervise. With the right structure in place, both parents can take turns and supervise in such a way that it does not overwhelm them.

   Without supervision, so many school children are unable to follow through even when they have the capacity to achieve set goals.

5. We have to steadily set specific milestones. The big goals are as good as the milestones. Milestones are the smaller steps that need to be accomplished in order for the big goal to be achieved. Milestones accomplished motivate people to go for bigger goals.

   For example, an A in final term grades as a goal in any given subject, needs to go with milestones such as prompt and well-done homework, A in test, A in projects. Sometimes, students take up to 6 test in a given term. A child can target to score 8/10 across board.

These are the build up to achieving set goals. Without identifying what the milestones are, it is near impossible to achieve the goals.

Set goals have to be comprehensive.

The most effective goals, apart from being realistic, are usually comprehensive in nature. They cover the before, during and post success aspects of our children's academic journey.

What do I mean by this?

Effective school goals must cover and invest in a child's self-belief, enthusiasm, academics and behavior.

This means that school goals should not shoot for grades alone.

a. Self-Belief Goals

When setting goals for school, addressing issues regarding our children's disposition to their personal capacities, subjects and teachers is of great importance. For example, there should be milestones such as asking more questions in class, overcoming the fear of certain subjects and teachers as well as overcoming long-held myths.

The self-belief goals should be empowered with affirmations that children say daily before going to school, while parents also work to help children address some of their misconceptions.

Self-belief goals are important because it is what a child believes that determines whether he or she will make an attempt towards success or not.

b. Enthusiasm Goals

Whatever we do as parents, we must infect our children with a love for school. We must inspire them to be motivated to learn. So many children are beginning to ask the question as to whether they need education to be successful. It is therefore pertinent to be proactive about helping them build a positive attitude towards school work.

How can you inspire enthusiasm in your child towards school work?

1. Demonstrate that their education is important to you. Pay school fees on time and be a part and parcel of the school decision-making process. Yes, attend PTA meetings or Parents' Forum no matter how boring they turn out to be. If you are going to be absent, please explain to your child.

2. You would periodically find yourself in situations where you feel the need to tell a teacher off. In those moments, try to bring yourself to a place of objectivity. Try not to verbally attack your children's teacher in front of your child. Do not do it in the absence of the teacher either.

Long after the foul mood is gone, you would expect your child to, in general, have the right attitude towards their teachers.

3. Make the effort to know your child's learning style, interests, talents and abilities. In knowing all of this, you would know how best to support and position the child for a rewarding experience at school.

    Sometimes, school can be most frustrating when children do not know how best to go about the challenging experiences they will be faced with. When parents know how to guide them into their most resourceful state, the children will achieve success which will motivate them to do more.

    For example, a parent who knows that his or her child is a visual learner – meaning he learns better when he watches TV or a screen. When that child is having difficulty grasping a concept, instead of wasting time blaming the child for not getting it, can ask the child or go along with child to look for online videos on the subject matter.

    In another case, a parent who knows that their child loves going to the cinema will know when to throw in a movie treat when the child has achieved a certain milestone like completing his or homework without being asked for the first half of the term.

In a third scenario, a parent who knows their child is brilliant at recollecting phone numbers, will use that fact to encourage their child to put some more effort when they are finding it difficult to grasp a mathematical concept.

When we know our children, we will know how best to support them.

4. As a parent, help your children make connections, between somewhat vague or abstract concepts taught at school, with real life experiences that they are most familiar with. This can happen over dinner time. During such moments, talk about what was taught, etc.

   Many times, in school, teachers teach by definitions and sometimes what is taught sounds abstract and does not make immediate meaning. However, when parents explain the same concept, using the everyday realities that they and their children can relate to, the children tend to understand better.

   Parents should therefore ask their children periodically about concepts they are finding difficult to understand.

   Some parents might say that it is what they par teachers for, but I can assure you, teachers teach a number of children at the same time. The personal attention that children need to blossom can only be given maximally by parents.

I am challenging you to make this sacrifice for your child because they are loaded with capacity. We do not want them to live a life far less than what they are capable off.

5. Provide rewards and tokens for appreciating the child for the effort. Sometimes, rewards are not necessarily money. A big warm hug, accompanying a parent somewhere, etc., can go a long way. Also, keeping track of newly formed habits that have been sustained over a period of time can be rewarded with something like a ticket to the movie or a chore-free day and even an extra 30 minutes of TV time on weekends.

6. Nothing beats parental involvement in inspiring a positive attitude towards school work. This can be substantiated by setting goals where parents have a role to play and the child has a role to play. This model of team execution of school goals enables a child to appreciate both parents' efforts and the entire education process.

c. Academic Goals

This is where we finally fire in and ask what the scores on the sheet are. Howbeit, as an educator, I can tell you that before grades, there are a couple of other questions and building blocks to put in place.

<u>Learning Goals</u>

Before grades, the first question to ask is: Did my child really learn at school today? Each school day builds on the previous school day. If a child did not learn or understand a concept on a certain day, moving on to future lessons can create a confusion in the entire learning process.

You should ask really simple questions such as:

- Can my child see the board from where he or she sits?

- Does he/she hear what the teacher says?

- Did they understand what the teacher said today?

While you may not be able to follow up each school day, you can teach your children to take personal responsibility for the whole experience, so that your children can also begin to ask themselves some of these questions.

Many of these questions can be addressed by understanding your child's learning style. Learning style talks about how the brain receives, processes and stores information. It defines a child's most conducive learning environment. Through understanding your child's learning style, you would be able to design the most suitable support for them.

No two children have the exact same learning style. We all learn differently.

There are four basic learning styles:

1. Visual learners.

2. Auditory learners.

3. Reading/writing-preference learners.

4. Kinesthetic learners (also known as "tactile learners").

Visual Learners

Visual learners are those who process and retain information best when they can see it. Visual learners often prefer to sit in the front of the class and "watch" the lecture closely. Often, these students will find that information makes more sense when it is explained with the aid of a chart or illustration.

Visual learners learn by sight, close their eyes to remember something and when they are bored, they look for something to watch. They are attracted to colors.

Study tips for visual leaners

They should color code their note books or jotters. Using color biros at different points of making notes in either their jotter or notebook, makes it more interesting to read.

1. They can create and use flash cards to remember important points while reading.

2. When reading, they should avoid distractions.

3. Draw symbols and pictures. Use symbols like exclamation points (for important information), question marks (for information that's confusing or that they need to study further) and stars (for information they understand fully).

4. Make outlines. Outlines are an excellent organizational tool for the visual learner. In an outline, they can structure a large amount of information using headings, subheadings, and bullet points. Mind maps sit in here perfectly.

Auditory Learners

An auditory learner depends on listening and speaking as a main way of learning. Auditory learners must be able to hear what is being said in order to understand and may have difficulty with instructions that are drawn but if the writing is in a logical order it can be easier to understand. They also use their listening and repeating skills to sort through the information sent to them. They are good listeners when people speak.

Study tips for auditory learners:

1. It is best that they sit where they can hear. At the same time, if they sit where there is whispering and noise, this can interfere with what the teacher is saying.

2. They study better when the read out aloud. Some parents have children who like to read out aloud, and usually they ask them to read to

themselves. Reading out loud helps them understand the material better.

3. They are good at explaining ideas out loud. It can be very helpful if they can use tape recorders to record themselves saying something or going over their notes and replay it later. There are recorder apps on everyday regular phones. When they read alone, they can record summaries for replay.

4. They could sit at the front of the classroom. Yes, they should find a spot around the front row so that they can hear every word of the lecture.

5. They should repeat facts with eyes closed. This technique will help them focus their attention on the auditory process, rather than any other visual stimuli that might be in front of them.

6. They should read assignments out loud. If they are given a homework assignment that involves reading a lengthy chapter, they should not feel like they're trapped into a silent reading session. Instead, they can curl up in their room or another study space and read aloud. (They can even make it interesting by using goofy voices.)

7. They should also participate in class discussions and speak out loud on the concepts that are being learned at each time.

Kinesthetic Learners

Also known as tactile learning, this is a learning style in which learning takes place when the students carry out physical activities, rather than listening to a lecture or watching demonstrations. A kinesthetic learner processes information best when he or she is physically engaged during the learning process.

Often, those with a kinesthetic learning style have a hard time learning through traditional lecture-based schooling because the body does not make the connection that they are doing something when they're listening without movement. Their brains are engaged, but their bodies are not, which makes it more difficult for them to process the information. Much of the time, they need to get up and move to put something into memory.

Essentially, a kinesthetic learns by touching and doing. They learn better when there is physical movement. They make a lot of hand gestures e.g. finger spelling. They easily imitate people.

Study tips for kinesthetic learners:

1. It's okay for them to chew gum, walk around and rock in a chair while studying or reading.

2. They should be encouraged to use flashcards and arrange them in groups to show relationships.

3. They should be allowed to take frequent breaks while studying.

4. They should stand up instead of sitting down. For kinesthetic learners, standing up will improve their comprehension and retention.

5. They should be allowed to tap a pencil, shake their foot, and hold on to something while learning.

Reading/Writing-Preference Learners

This is a learning style where individuals are able to absorb and retain the most information through reading and writing text, versus imagery and symbolism. The primary means of learning for reading/writing learners are through reading lecture notes, writing essays, reading through textbooks, writing notes, etc. The reading/writing learners prefer to have information displayed in word and text form, as it is easiest for them to absorb and store for future use.

Study tips for reading/writing-preference learners:

1. They should study alone in quiet areas to avoid distractions.

2. They should stick to the traditional teaching and learning methods of school, as these works best for them. These include reading textbooks, taking notes, re-writing notes, re-reading notes, etc.

3. Encourage them to take LOTS of notes. Keeping them organized with sub-headings,

bullet points, and lists will also help for absorbing and retaining the information to use later on.

4. They should endeavor to keep all their jottings and use them productively. Combining their jottings with main notes can help them create a collective input of information.

5. Read their notes over (silently) again and again.

6. They should also turn diagrams and charts into words. By recreating them under a different format, they will be learning about the diagrams and charts at the same time.

Please note:

1. Many of the study tips should be explored primarily at home.

2. There are research findings that show that teaching children in their preferred learning style is not as effective. So, while classroom work will continue to vary in approach, a child's personal study should be patterned after their predominant style.

3. No one is totally of any learning style. Everyone is a combination of all three in varying proportions.

   To conduct a learning style test for your children or yourself, please visit www.educationplanner.org

Growth goals

This is where, as parents, we pursue personal improvements that may or may not be reviewed by a teacher. This is where home practice comes in. There will be times when our children are falling behind in one thing or the other. Since the classroom is not designed to wait for any one, while the teacher keeps laying on subsequent lessons, at home, a child should be made to practice and practice concepts that they found somewhat difficult in class.

I remember when one of my daughters had an issue with division. I would gather practice sheet from different websites and then make her practice and practice. Regardless of what was homework from school, I made her practice divisions over and over.

Technology makes it so much easier. I am a subscriber to a website called www.education.com and I get unlimited free downloads on different subjects and different topics. Many times, I love the unique ways that they introduce concepts and I have found their resources helpful.

Some websites offer the opportunity for a child to listen to someone else teach a concept that they may not have understood at school while others use gaming to teach concepts. This allows children of varying learning styles to find approaches that they are most suited to.

What are other sites you can go to for printable worksheets and even online practice?

Disclaimer: This is in no way an endorsement of any of the below listed websites. I have not used all of them. Parents are advised to thoroughly review each of these websites before exposing their child to them.

1. www.khanacademy.org

2. www.education.com

3. www.scholastic.com

4. www.starfall.com

5. http://pbskids.org/games/

6. www.abcya.com

7. www.funbrain.com

8. www.lightupyourbrain.com

9. www.prongo.com

10. www.factmonster.com

11. www.multiplication.com

12. http://www.arcademics.com/games/

13. http://www.primarygames.com/

14. http://www.bbc.co.uk/schools/games/

15. http://www.poptropica.com/

16. http://kids.nationalgeographic.com/

17. http://mrnussbaum.com/

18. http://www.sheppardsoftware.com/

19. http://labyrinth.thinkport.org/www/

20. http://electrocity.co.nz/

21. http://www.gamesforchange.org/play/fatworld/

22. http://3rdworldfarmer.com/

23. http://www.nothingbutnets.net/its-easy-to-help/game.html

24. http://www.stopdisastersgame.org/en/home.html

25. http://educationalgames.nobelprize.org/educational/

26. http://brightstorm.com/

27. http://thefutureschannel.com/

28. www.study.com

29. https://www.w3schools.com (Coding)

30. https://ed.ted.com

31. https://www.codecademy.com

32. http://www.openculture.com

There are also highly educational YouTube Channels such as:

1. Smithsonian Channel

2. The Brain Scoop

3. Houston Zoo

4. WordWorldPBS

5. Sesame Street

6. TED-Ed

7. Smart Girls

8. SoulPancake

9. SciShow

10. It's Okay to Be Smart

11. Smarter Everyday

12. Physics Girl

13. Minute Physics

14. Crash Courses

15. Kurzgesagt – In a Nutshell

16. Reactions – Everyday Chemistry

17. Asap Science

I have always thought that more and more parents should embrace technology as an aid to learning rather than exploring the use of technology for entertainment purposes mainly.

The 21st century has brought with it several devices, platforms and so on and so forth, that can actually aid learning.

Dear parent, all you need to do now is ensure you always have a pack of A4 papers, a small desktop printer and resources listed from the above sites to help your child catch up when they are lagging behind and even when they need to read ahead. I am so certain that the resources they will access online may be far ahead of their classroom experience.

Growth goals of setting up a home library.

At the beginning of this book, I spent time speaking about the role that spellings and grammar play in the final grades children make. Learning without being able to express it will undermine the opportunities that your child can take advantage of.

A major growth goal to set is to help your child build and improve on their vocabulary which can be achieved by frequent reading. Setting up a home library and inspiring a reading culture in your home will make all the difference.

To begin this, make a monthly budget of how much you plan to invest in buying books. Nothing is too big or too small. I recommend that you start with an amount that you can follow through sustainably. If your budget is too small to get a decent number of books per time, don't worry, 2 books a month is a great start. Otherwise you can also explore buying used books.

Also, design an incentive system for reading. You may need a little budget for this too or totally design a system that may not require money per se.

Here are some ideas for inspiring reading as a culture in your home:

1. Have a family reading night, where everyone reads.
2. Have the children read non-academic books for 30 minutes each day.
3. Reward the children for not being reminded to go and read.
4. Take the children to a library in the neighbourhood.
5. Set up a nice reading area that is cozy and very attractive to the children.
6. Buy titles that are of interest to your children at the onset. Also, find what format of books they prefer. My first daughter has started showing interest in reading books off a computer.
7. You can plan a reading picnic with a basket of snacks and drinks the children really love. It can be a family tradition.

You may also have other ideas or stumble on other ideas on how to make reading fun.

Other growth opportunities:

Growth at school also involves improving the

children's handwriting. This is super easy to do. You can download handwriting worksheets from online and have the child go over for a few minutes a day or a couple of days each week.

Please legibility is different from beauty. Try not to make the child write like you. Set the goals of legible writing and allow the child set their target for beautiful writing.

When thinking about the opportunities for improvement for your child and how much commitment you have to make, imagine everyday that you are raising an Einstein. Think about everything you gave to do as efforts on getting your Einstein into shape.

Remember, that your child is created on purpose and through these routines, you are teaching your child the practice of discipline, self-improvement, growth and the very special lesson for everyone of us, especially those of us in Africa which is that 'success is predictable'.

<u>Grade goals</u>

For us to achieve our big grade goals, we begin to track from note completions, performance in test, performance in homework and then performance in examinations.

Parents need to create and maintain regimens that ensure the child is completing their homework. If you start out early building homework into a strict routine, it may be easier to follow. By strict routine, I mean creating something that may look like this: after school you bath, eat, do homework before watching one hour of television. Please, don't leave it open-ended. When you leave it open to children, they will always have challenges prioritizing.

School projects should be taken seriously.

As a result of what combines to make up final term grades, school goals must incorporate:

1. Note completion goals. Always include the days that, as a parent, you will review notes.

2. Prompt homework submission.

3. Proper and neatly done homework.

4. Preparation for test every other week with or without teachers' notice.

5. Anticipated grades for tests.

6. Anticipated grades for projects.

7. Anticipated grades for note completion.

8. Anticipated grades for examinations.

In summary, here are some hacks for supporting our children through school:

1. <u>Imagine right now that you are opening a new chapter in your child's academic life.</u>

Picture it. Picture a whole new beginning. One that is

not full of complaints and continual failure. One that is full of brilliance. Close your eyes now and picture you and your child starting a new beginning.

Picture a new beginning. But more than just dream, dare to create a new story with a happy ending. See your child actually succeed. Yes, that child you are worried about.

2. <u>Redefine success for your child.</u>

So, my daughter struggled to read at the beginning. At this point there was no need benchmarking her against her peers or her elder sister. I had to redefine what success meant along the way. My goal was not to see her top her class; my priority was to set growth goals for her. I created private practice sessions at home and allowed her watch herself do things she ordinarily could not do in class setting.

The confidence of achieving during private practice soon started paying off at school where she was able to make meaningful contributions to the point of being able to read and prepare herself for tests on her own in a single school year.

In other words, I created a parallel curriculum of things I wanted her to be able to do on her own by the end of that term. And which if she succeeded at, I would be comfortable.

When I went for her open day, her teacher said she had improved in sitting still in class but that she needed improvement in her handwriting. So, I mentioned to her that she didn't need to be worried about her handwriting because it was a next term's goal.

The reason is that handwriting was not on our first term goals but reading fluently, paying attention in class, and doing number transitions such as 19 to 20, 29 to 30 etc.

When you begin benchmarking your child's performance by your own standards, then you and your child will make a lot more progress which will be very encouraging to your child and impact on their performance. That way expectations are realistic and a child is not overburdened in the process.

3. <u>Ask for your child's scheme of work.</u>

When you are pushing your children to study without knowing what is exactly on the scheme, it is akin to flying blind.

For starters, many struggling kids can be overwhelmed. If parents could know what they would be learning for each week and just talked about these topics and explained them in simple and relatable ways, then you would have demystified the concept before or while they are taught at school.

And demystifying here would mean explaining the concepts in ways that they can totally relate with.

4. <u>Create routines at home and stick with them.</u>

Routines here include bedtime routine, homework routine, TV routine, etc. The lack of predictability means anything goes and their priorities are steadily misplaced.

Design what happens after school, and after that, and after that and what time bed time is.

5.   <u>Incentivize studying.</u>

Your child has different levels of study experiences you should supervise and incentivize. Yes, celebrate little wins.

<u>Asking questions in class</u>: Require of your child to ask questions, provide answers, make comments and seek clarification in class.

<u>Ensure that their notes are up to date:</u> (For teens) Ask for their timetable to be placed in the open. And stop by very often without notice to check whether their notes are up to date by just glancing on the time table and asking to see the notes for the day.

<u>Ensure that homework is done daily</u>: Ask and take a look.

<u>Create a reading policy for your home</u>: For example, everyone is required to read for two hours daily, etc.

Then reward them for adherence. Reward them with simple and big things to encourage the behavior. After a while, they will do it even without an incentive.

Typical incentives:

- Bonus screen time (15 – 30 minutes) This could be extra TV or Game time. The caveat though is that anything over two hours a day is detrimental to a child's health.

- Make favorite meal

- Go on a dinner date with mummy or daddy

- Ice cream

- A visit to grannies'

- Cinema treats

- Day Off Chores

6. <u>Fill your homes with resources such as books, books and more books.</u>

Yes, buy story books, fact books, academic and non-academic books. Raise kids who read for fun. It builds their curiosity, sharpens their mind towards learning and gives them the vocabulary to express what they know

A library full of books will do more for a child than a wardrobe full of shoes. And if you can, do both.

7. <u>Create room for your child to practice and practice.</u>

If your child has handwriting issues, get a 20-leaves exercise book and let them practice. Also, have them write several lines a day continually until they master it. Practice makes perfect.

If its counting, additions or subtractions, if possible,

photocopy their homework pages, so that after they have submitted, they can do and redo until they master the concepts they are learning.

To support this, you can look online for worksheets and resources that you can also print so that you can have a variety. Use any of the websites I had mentioned before or any other website, along with YouTube channels to search for videos on topics your child may be having difficulty in.

8. <u>Speak only wholesome words.</u>

Speak the right words to your children. And have them speak the right words to themselves daily. This can be referred to as affirmations.

9. <u>Find out what your child's learning style is and support them in studying in that manner.</u>

- Key Points

- School success does not happen by mere wishing. Effective goal setting is the first step to bringing it together.
- Effective goals must be realistic. It must take into consideration the school's curriculum, a child's pace as well as state clearly defined milestones.
- What our children believe about themselves, their capacity, their teachers and subjects will also influence performance.
- An effective goal must clearly specify the role that parents will play in bringing the goal to fruition.

CHAPTER FOUR
RE-CREATING SCHOOL SUCCESS

School success can be recreated over and over again. There is a science to it. A child who has no learning disability and has an understanding of his/her learning style enough to maximize it, can determine that he/she will be an alpha student at any level of their education.

The science is about creating culture, beliefs, practices and habits that are directed towards success. I will essentially pull out different things I have talked about in the course of writing this book. Students who repeatedly practice these things will repeatedly recreate success.

This chapter is specifically written to be read along with parents. I really do not mind the entire book to be given to children to read so that both parents and children are on the same page.

1. Write legibly.

Write in such a manner that your teachers can easily read your handwriting. It does not need to be anything aesthetic. Write boldly. Put the tip of the pen down on the paper. Practice writing over and over to improve, if you have trouble writing legibly.

2. Do not miss lessons.

During lessons take notes. Not just lesson notes but

take note of explanations that your teacher gives. Take note of questions others are asking and how your teacher is answering them. You too ask questions.

3. Do not miss lessons.

You can be physically present but mentally absent. Let your friends know that you can play together after the lesson is over. Try to take your mind off the movie you watched or the person that said something nasty to you. Try not to daydream during lessons. Imagine that every word your teacher says will help you.

4. Read at the end of each day.

Spend time reading notes of lessons that you were taught and also reading ahead for subsequent topics. Many schools today give students the scheme of work. This should help you plan ahead.

5. When you read ensure that you completely understand.

Create a means of testing your understanding. You can pre-set questions before you start reading that you will answer after reading. You can record a discussion in a recorder and listen to it over and over. You can ask your parent or sibling to ask you random questions at the end of your reading session. That usually really helps.

6. Design a reading timetable that is realistic for success.

Give subjects that are bulky and require some practice more attention but not all the attention. When you do, be consistent.

7. Find out what your preferred learning style is and maximize it.

Yes, follow the study tips provided as a guide for how you study outside the classroom.

Ask your parents to visit www.educationplanner.org so that you can take a learning style test and ascertain what your learning style is.

See page 54 -59 for learning style tips.

8. Pack everything you need for the next school day on the night before.

Pack homework, requirements, textbooks, notebooks, snacks, drinks, water, etc. Also bring out uniforms, socks, shoes on the night before. Clean everything that needs to be cleaned ahead of the next day of school.

9. Plan for your grades.

End of term grades are a combination of tests, assignments, projects and examinations. Be diligent in completing homework. Anticipate test. Stay ready for examinations.

10. During examinations read questions properly.

Follow written instructions and maximize time given to you to write your examinations. Always remember to write your name on your answer sheet.

11. Embrace learning.

Every time a test script or homework script is returned, always look out for and study the teacher's remark on your scripts. Take note of questions you scored poorly as well as question you scored highly. Look out for the correct answers to learn from questions you scored poorly and review how you answered the questions that you scored highly. Learn from both your successes and your failures.

12. Embrace rigor.

Tough topics are as tough as you make them. Break them down. Start with what you know. Ask for help but ask for help that shows you how to do it and not help that does it for you. Don't ask for help in the examinational hall.

See page 22 – 27 for 'How to handle rigor'

13. Be a self-starter.

There would be days that you are not in the mood at all. Learn how to at least take down notes during lessons you do not find interesting at all.

14. Be a self-grower.

Throughout the course of school, you would find that the class hardly ever waits for you. If you notice an area that you are unable to perform as much as your teacher expects for you to, don't wait for the teacher to come and teach you. Commit to your own improvement. Ask classmates who are really good at it to help you. Create moments of private practice. Keep practicing until you are comfortably good.

Ask your parents to help you find safe online platforms that you can go over the concepts on.

15. Take English Language seriously.

It does not matter what you want to say, if you do not have the words or the right words to get your message across, what you are saying will lose its meanings. Apply the things you are being taught in English language to other subjects whenever you are required to answer questions.

Read novels, newspapers, articles, blogs, etc. Build your vocabulary by reading online and in prints. Keep a dictionary handy.

Then practice writing. Take up writing challenges online and build your vocabulary as well as your writing speed. Do not shy away from taking part in essay writing competitions. Look out for competition announcements on your parent's newspapers. You never know, there may be exciting prizes to win and you could just bring it home.

- Key Points

- Luck does not count for school success. There has to be a life style of intentionality.
- School success happens to be predictable.

CHAPTER FIVE
PREPARING TEENS FOR UNIVERSITY SUCCESS

For many of our teenagers, a university education may be the very first opportunity of living away from home. That in itself is very exciting. Yes, it would the first time they live away from the prying, over protective eyes of their parents. Just like with going away to boarding, the 'sudden' liberty can compete with paying attention and following through with school work, especially in the first year of school.

Unlike secondary school, the university final grades begin to count from the very first year. What this means is that a child you suddenly becomes super serious, super responsible in second year, would still suffer the consequence of a weak performance at the time they graduate.

In what ways can we as parents help our teens prepare and adjust appropriately and soon enough when they resume school at the university?

Ensure that what they are going to study is truly what they want to study or what they believe it is.

Many teenagers have an assumption about what certain courses entail and sooner or later, they find that it may not be the way they had expected. This eventually affects their commitment to school work.

On the other hand, many of them are going in to study what parents want. In many ways, they do not feel connected to the course and may just turn to many things to keep sane while doing these courses.

One way of addressing this is through volunteering and internships. If your child has an interest in a certain field, it's important to expose them to companies who work in that field. It can help them appreciate the field more, understand different aspects of the industry. It can also help them understand what it is lecturers will be teaching. On the other hand, if what they have in mind is totally different from what they experience and they do not feel connected to it, then they are empowered to make an informed decision.

Many parents try to suggest courses for legitimate reasons. At this time, I am not talking about when parents say, we must have a lawyer, doctor, engineer or accounting. Today's surge is for children to go into ICT. Children are created on purpose; I recommend parents pay attention to their children's wiring as they work with the children to make career decisions.

Many parents see what their child can be but perceive that their child is settling, some actually watch their children trying to join the bandwagon and know there is a need for them to be a voice of reason. This for me is legitimate. However, before you send such a child to university for that course that you think is right for them, ensure that there is a buy in. This means that it will be more of conversations than instructions,

Let them know why you think what you do, open up conversations with them and while you are at it, do listen to them as well.

Have them connect to a mentor.

Whatever their field of study is, let them find a mentor or someone who they admire strongly in that field of study. I usually recommend one mentor they can walk up to and have conversations with and another who is a public figure.

The public figure could be someone they can follow online and see their everyday work pattern, goals, projects and priorities.

LinkedIn today is a professional platform for following industry leaders and influencers.

Seeing people who have gone ahead in the fields can be a huge source of encouragement to the teens.

Have teens follow the ideas in this book.

This book has talked a lot about building success-oriented school behavior. It really does not matter what level of education that they are in, it's the same principles.

A teen who has mastered using these principles in secondary school will be totally ready to drive themselves towards school success with minimal or no supervision.

Let them learn about the university grading system.

This really eludes many young people. Please get seniors and other graduates to break it down. What it takes to graduate with a first class, a second class upper as well as a second class lower. Sometimes in the cause of this kinds of conversations, teens learn about how difficult it can be to access certain opportunities on certain grade levels.

It is better for them to have the grades and not need the opportunities available than for them to really want the opportunities but realize that they cannot access these opportunities as a result of their grades.

Give the teens liberty before they leave home.

Yes, let them have a semblance of independence before leaving for university. Let them drive, if they fall within the legal age to drive. Essentially, give them both adult-ish rights and responsibilities.

This will serve two purposes: first, it will allow you see their tendencies, so that you can nudge them here and there. It can show you areas to help them reform what they think about certain things.

Secondly, it will also give them the impression that they are already treated as adults. This will reduce the tendency for them to want to implode at school. Many times, teens that are under lock and key at home usually go wild at school and eventually live double lives at home and at school.

That can be a very dangerous place to be.

Give teens responsibility before they leave home.

Chores are always a life saver. Responsibilities are skill builders. Give teens something they can be responsible for. In the house it can be managing maintenance, coordinating pantry refill etc.

All of this will always involve them setting goals, mobilizing resources, working against timelines etc. All of these shapes their behavior and patterns.

Teens that are served until the last moment will be overwhelmed with the liberty that they would find at school.

- Key Point

* Many teens underperform because of lack of information and/or poor sense of personal responsibility. We can bridge the gap by helping provide knowledge and experiences before they leave home for university.

CONCLUSION:
21ST CENTURY EDUCATION PRIORITY

At the beginning, I shared a typical example of how learning and grades sometimes do not meet. I mentioned how a child who may have learned a subject but has the inability to express in written examinations and in the end, it does not amount to great grades. I also shared about children who are really brilliant as well who cheat the system and themselves in the process.

They memorize most concepts, deliver on teacher's terms and earn the grades but soon after the examination, they have very little retention of concepts they have learned.

For example, a child who loves biology, understands biology but is poor in written English especially spelling, has illegible handwriting and as such never scores above a certain score. And another child who does not like biology but can commit time to memorize, writes well and scores far better in the test.

The truth is that, our children need to master concepts as well as learn how to effectively express them. This is the core. This is the standard. Howbeit, for 21st century success, the real success is the child with mastery of concepts. Today, he would type more often than he would write. He/she can install a grammar software on his laptop, which will edit his written communication on the go.

His or her mastery of the concept is irreplaceable. Through the mastery, such a child will understand his work and perform far better than those peers, who are great test takers and always focus more on passing the test than actually learning. That child will have sustained interest to keep learning and adapting to industry changes.

Should he/she decide to venture, they will be more resourceful.

The 21st century successful kid is a pro. He or she needs to master concepts. We must help them develop the self-drive towards success. Of which, if they do, they can apply these self-drive principles in other areas of their lives. School should be a preparation ground that instils values that tend towards success.

School work, adequately organized, will teach a child planning, prioritization, self-appraisal, how to process feedback while helping them discover their areas of interest.

Too many students drift through school without discovering their talents and while our curriculum could do better in facilitating these changes, I would like to see more families emphasizing more than grades while not undermining grades at the same time.

Let us take the recommendations in this book and apply them to our children's lives. The recommendations here are guaranteed to result in success – school success, life success and, ultimately, 21st century success!

IRENE BANGWELL

AFTERWORD

I love the fact that the author of this very instructive manual on how to succeed in school uses her academic life story, starting from Primary school to University, to cleverly illustrate many germane and highly critical issues concerning why some children succeed at school while others don't. The significant role played by circumstance, attitude and approach is not left out.

In this beautiful piece, the unassailable benefits of having a watchful parent around, a favourite mantra of all educators, is further reaffirmed as we learn how Irene blossomed under the mother's tutelage, whenever the mother was at home. Thereby confirming the generally accepted position that teachers cannot do it alone.

The positive habits, behavior and subsequent characteristics of those who succeed at school are well documented here. By refusing to limit her observations/interrogation to purely academic activities and casting out her net to include often overlooked activities, she quite successfully convinces the reader of the nexus between behavior and result.

The right habits quite naturally prepare and organise a child's mind in a way which leads to academic success. Moving on from this, Irene also touches on the age long debate of the value of education by comparing the child who is intrinsically motivated vis-à-vis the child who is extrinsically motivated. The extrinsically motivated child is persuaded to study because of the promise of instant reward, which means he or she is not self-driven to succeed. The intrinsically motivated child however, is self-driven by the allure of success. He or she recognizes the long-term value of education and is happy to delay gratification. Like the author points out, such children don't need to be constantly goaded before they pick up their books to study.

Individuals who view education as merely an exercise to make you clever and nothing else and who fail to see the instrumental value it bestows, are far less likely to be intrinsically motivated. Subsequently, they shouldn't realistically be expected to make many useful contributions to society.

However, those who even at an early age understand the inevitable role education will play for them to enjoy future success in life, will be driven from within themselves. It is therefore important for both parents and teachers to paint this clear picture for children to whom this stark reality may not readily come to mind.

Good learning habits, orderly and forward-thinking preparation which the author strongly recommends would stand one in good stead for success, no matter the career path one eventually decides to follow.

Irene's early learning experiences subtly make a case for school learning in one's mother tongue, at least at the introductory stage. Scientific studies have shown that countries where pupils are taught in their native language at the early stages of schooling, tend to perform better.

Education, though informal at the initial stage, actually begins from home so the constant switch from one language to the other when they commence school can result in a slight interruption of intellectual development. Learning in the same language in which they communicate at home makes the switch from home to school seamless. However, research has shown that children at the formative age can learn as many languages as possible because their brain at that stage is absorbent.

Of equal importance is the author's perhaps more pointed recommendations for both parents and schools to allow children to remain in classes appropriate to their age. In the UK as well as in some other countries, this is a must, for the simple reason that children have more to benefit when grouped with children of similar level of physical, mental and psychological development. Cases of bullying, intimidation and oppression are likely to be fewer and further in between and this speaks to better results academically and otherwise.

This body of work is not the culmination of a mere mundane study but of rigorous, painstaking and altogether novel research. Managing to keep it both surprisingly specific and comprehensive in it's scope, those smart enough to religiously follow its explicit counsel are unlikely to put a foot wrong.

Truth be told, I wish such a guide like this was made available to my parents and I when I was growing up.

Maureen Ihonor
Immediate Past Director of Education,
Corona School's Trust Council
Founder,
Cedar Ridge Educational and Library Services Ltd.

ABOUT THE AUTHOR

Irene Bangwell is the Co-founder of KNOSK, an education innovation company that focuses on actionizing learning, education research and providing parenting education.

She writes, creates new tools, and designs programs that make learning spaces more empowering for children and teens. She is the designer of the Education Innovation Map, amongst other education management tools.

She has authored other parenting books including; **Raising Kids Who Are Influence Proof, Moving from Overwhelmed to Overwhelm, 12 Things Every Parent Should Know** and **Raising Girls and the Boys who would love them.**

She has worked as an on-air parenting coach since 2010 and has mentored and continues to mentor hundreds of teens since 2008.

Irene Bangwell is married to Kingsley Bangwell and together they have two amazing daughters, Briona and Elena who love God, arts and want to solve global problems.

To learn more about KNOSK;
Visit: www.knoskeducation.com
Email: ask@knosk.com.ng
Phone: +234 9033338510.

www.ingramcontent.com/pod-product-compliance
Lightning Source LLC
Chambersburg PA
CBHW061432160726
47995CB00003B/858